ALICE MUNRO:A CONTEMPORARY LEGENDARY WRITER

SHORT STORIES OF ALICE MUNRO:A STUDY

DR.INDRA SINGH TOMAR

XpressPublishing
An imprint of Notion Press

XpressPublishing
An Imprint of Notion Press

Old No. 38, New No. 6
McNichols Road, Chetpet
Chennai - 600 031

First Published by Notion Press 2020
Copyright © Dr.indra Singh Tomar 2020
All Rights Reserved.

ISBN 978-1-64869-115-7

To my Grand Mother and Grand Father

Contents

Acknowledgements

These words would be a mere formality but are an expression of sentiments from the core of my heart. The hard work, which spanned over years and culminated into this book, is the end result of the blessings of the Almighty. On the successful completion of my book, I would like to thank my friend, **Dr. Kulraj Vyas** whose inspirational guidance, constructive criticism and supportive approach made it possible to complete this work. His sagacious guidance and keen insight helped me to remain focused whenever I was imperceptibly going off-track.

I also express my heartfelt sense of indebtedness to Dr.B.K. Sharma, Professor P.G. department of English studies and research M.L.B. Govt. college of Excellence and Dr. Archana Agarwal, HOD, M.L.B. Govt. College of Excellence, Gwalior, Prof. P.R. Pande, M.L.B. Govt. College of Excellence, Gwalior, who have been the never ending source of motivation and enlightenment in my research pursuit.

My heartfelt thanks are due to my family for the co-operation and help they extended to me throughout my research work. I am deeply grateful to the pious blessings of grand mother **Smt. Renuka Bai, Shri Suresh Singh Tomar** my respected father, **Smt. Mira Devi**my beloved mother and my uncles **Shri Mahesh Singh Tomar**& **Shri Hanumant Singh Bhadoriya**. I am equally indebted to my brothers **Shri Ramesh Singh Tomar, Shri Dwarikadhish Singh Tomar** younger brother**Devendra**, my wife **Smt. Poonam Tomar**and my friends **Mohit Arora, Lisa Jellifo**who have taught me to be hardworking, consistent and farsighted, without their support and help I would not have been able to complete this book.

My thanks are further due to my friends and the rest of whom I have forgotten to mention here but who supported and cooperated with me in many ways towards the completion of this book.

(Dr. Indra Singh Tomar)

Date:03/03/2020
Place: Gwalior

CHAPTER ONE

Short story and her life

The Canadian short story which began to develop as a national genre in the decade of 1890s is still a fairly recent literary phenomenon, having gained more popularity in recent times. Its most important model of growth was the American short story, which by the end of nineteenth century was far more nurtured by representative writers such as Nathaniel Hawthorne and Edgar Allan Poe.

The 1920s can be termed as the starting point of the modernist short story writing. In this decade there was a general lack of appreciation for Canadian short story along with limited publication facilities, which caused this genre to have rather an obstructive start. It was only in the 1960s the period of, the so-called Canadian Renaissance when most writers from the 1920s were able to publish their work in Canada. The flourishing print industry developed in Canada, which helped the short story to grow through multiple publications in magazines, collections and anthologies. At present the short story can be acknowledged to be the leading genre of Canadian literature.

In comparison to the American short story, postmodernist shorter fiction did never flourished in Canada. It rather combined such experimental, deconstructive, and self-referential features with the traditional Canadian interest in realist representation. The Canadian short story is characterized by an apparent predominance of modernist and neo-realist narratives over outright anti-realist, postmodernist styles.

In recent times three most known English-Canadian short story writers are female: Margaret Atwood, Mavis Gallant and Alice Munro, of which Munro exclusively writes short stories. Her grand success in global scenario has helped to raise the profile of the Canadian short story. Munro's attraction to the short-story format is linked to her specific writing aesthetics, which emphasizes the fluidity, incompleteness, variability, and the ultimate peculiarity of human behavior through the use of explanatory gaps, the construction of words alongside the contrasting of complex interpretations, proximity of past and present, the contrasting deferral of fixed meanings, etc.

Modern Canadian short story can be marked first by its diversity and vitality, since almost every Canadian writer has made a contribution to the short story. Secondly, by the high number of short-story cycles bring it closer to the novel; and the third specific feature of the Canadian fiction is its tradition of storytelling.

Alice Munro is regarded as one of the best short story writers in the world and has been crucial in making short-story writing respectable in Canada. Moreover, she has been included in the 2010 Times magazine's 100 Most Influential people. She won the Noble Prize in the year 2013 for her contribution to the short story.

Too Much Happiness is her seventh short story collection, published at the age of seventy eight and forty years after her first collection appeared. Throughout long literary career, her style and themes have not changed a lot, although in her stories, she tends to emphasize more on the sufferings, constrains and loneliness of old age, and the way her narrators tell a story based on memories from their youth. Thus, she has gained new perspectives of time and space as her characters have grown older along with Munro herself, reflecting on their personal histories. In order to know what it is that makes Munro's short stories so remarkable, some theoretical background will be provided, such as a short history of English-Canadian short story, as well as some features of it. Furthermore, although Munro is famous for her realistic style, a close examination of Canadian postmodernism will prove that Munro's style is a typical Canadian one, with an unbelievable narrative and gothic connotations.

In order to appreciate Alice Munro's works, we need to go through the geography of Canada. Certainly, Munro's narratives are connected to specific geographical locations, for she is fascinated by local history and geography and her stories offer social maps of small-town life for example- rural Ontario, though like women's gossip they also narrate socially unspeakable events, those Open Secrets which she focuses on telling and which are absolutely off the map. Reading Munro's stories is to discover the pleasure of seeing two worlds at once: an ordinary everyday life and the shadowy map of another fictitious or secret world.

Munro describes the familiar places where she grew up in the 1930s and 1940s and where she still lives. That map of Canada can be seen by locating a group of small town in southwestern Ontario (Wingham, Clinton, and Goderich on Lake Huron) we would describe Munro's geographical territory. Though her stories make some trips outside to Toronto and to Vancouver, and later to Australia and Scotland and even Albania, her work is confined to a long tradition of Canadian small-town fiction where anywhere else is outsider and alien, be it as near as Toronto or as far away as Sydney, Australia. Munro left her home town when she went to university in London, a few hours' ride away; then she married and went to live in British Columbia for twenty years where her three children were born and where she and her husband ran a bookshop in Victoria. Recollecting those days she writes, *"All through the 50s I was living in a dormitory suburb, having babies, and writing wasn't part of the accepted thing for a girl or a woman to do at that time either, but it never occurred to me that I should stop".*[5]

Significantly, Munro focuses on the fact that she had gone out for writing stories all through that period. Twenty-one short stories were published before her first collection *Dance of the Happy Shades* published in 1968, and it won the prestigious Governor General's Award. Her first two books were published while she was in British Columbia, then in the early 1970s her marriage broke up thereafter she returned to Ontario, where she engaged herself in creative writing and still lives. With her growing international popularity she began to travel to England and Scotland, then to Australia in 1979 and 1980, and she celebrated her fiftieth birthday in China with a group of Canadian writers. These pleasing moments are reflected in an occasional widening of reference in her stories from *The Moons of Jupiter* onwards.

Some critics often rage queries regarding the autobiographical nature of her stories to which she has replied: *"In incident, no ... in emotion, completely".*[6]The answer would seem to be rather more confusing as she reveals in her 1982 essay *What Is Real?*, where she explained how she writes a story:

Some of the material I may have lying around already, in memories and observations, and some I invent, and some I have to go diligently looking for (factual details), while some is dumped in my lap (anecdotes and bits of speech). I see how this material might go together to make the shape I need, and I try it.[7]

In her third short story collection there is a story entitled *Material* in which she describes the relation between real life and fictional world. Herein she narrates the story of an unlucky woman called Dotty in Vancouver, from the contrasting viewpoints of a male and female writer.

What is the secret of the enduring popularity and appeal of the short story of Alice Munro, particularly the influence she exerts on an international readership? It is clearly Munro's well knit plot and the documentary quality which is the secret of her international appeal. She creates locations and characters so exactly that readers are amazed as if it is happening with their own life. Yet at the same time, these stories could be anywhere - any small town, any farmhouse:

Her female protagonists have a distinct double awareness of community values and of what else goes on outside those confines. They are deeply attracted by dark holes and by unscripted spaces with their sensational and discreditable stories of transgression and desire. Munro registers this ambiguity of vision very clearly in *Lives* of *Girls* and *Women* when describing her adolescent narrator's home town of Jubilee: *"People's live in Jubilee, as elsewhere, were dull, simple, amazing, unfathomable, deep caves paved with kitchen linoleum"*.[9]Such observation exposes the limits of realistic fiction by its challenge to domestic premises indicating what is usually hidden or unspoken within the acknowledged social order of small-town life.

Munro's short stories are frequently introduced as gossip and they circulate as gossip; they are complex interwoven fragments, full of glimpses of parallel lives and silent knowledge of women bodies. They delineate casualties of the female lie, of love stories and failed romantic fantasies. Adolescent female characters have passion for more glamorous narratives than their day to day live contain. Munro takes up the traditional subjects of women's fiction, keeping their imaginative appeal and power in mind. Her stories considerably alter female plots so that they become stories of traps and escape with women seeing themselves as spies or aliens, and where secrecy and silence are strategies of camouflaged resistance to conventional social decorum. These stories have a positive function as women's counter-discourse, suggesting alternative map for women's destinies beyond traditional patterns of masculine authority and gender stereotyping, drawing new ways to delineate women's differences - not only from men but also from one another across gap of generation, class and education.

As a female writer Munro is always sensitive about the issues related to girls and women. She stresses that female subjectivity is intimately bound up with sexuality and desire, and the contradictoriness of women's desires is one of her major topics. Instead, she provides the paradoxical experiential evidence with which theorists are seeking to come to terms as she explores sexual difference from within - in women's fantasies and in the dynamic relations between women and men as well as between women themselves. Her stories present unlimited celebrations and revisions of female romantic fantasies with all their urgent sexual hunger, their perplexing contradictions and disappointments, and their disdain of age and experience. She does not depict Harlequin romances or soft porn though she comprehends precisely their appeal.

The raw material of the psyche is the same, as that narrator recalls us: *"I can't apologize for the banality of my dreams".[14]* Romantic fantasy provides escape though it is not merely about escapism; nor is it simply a *"how-to book for women who lack power' though that access to power through love and sex is important too".[15]* Such fantasy also provides an inner space from which to imagine alternative life stories and to renegotiate connections, at least in imagination, between private and public worlds. This is the secret world where women explore their deepest desires and fears, and only here do Munro's protagonists perforate some of the mysteries of their lives and personal relationships. Their fantasies dramatize women's parallel unlived lives of dreamed- of possibilities, culminating in a late story like *Carried Away* in *Open Secrets* where an old woman comes across the ghost of a man who has been dead for years and he declares his love for her in a magical moment of radiant vanishing consolations. But for all their glimmering promises, fantasies always turn out to be unreliable structures, rickety inventions or sudden holes and impromptu tricks. They are untrustworthy but they are also infinitely tempting because they offer at least partial maps of the feminine fancy.

In a 1982 interview she spoke about the initial rush of excitement before beginning to write a story, *"When it hits me ... I think that beginning perception, that first perception, is the total moment and from then on there's all this work."[18]* In her story *White Dump* she makes a similar comment about a love affair: *"I think the best part is always right at the beginning ... Perhaps just when it flashes on you what's possible. That may be the best".[19]*

Munro learned a great amount from Welty's stories in *The Golden Apples* which she read and reread when it appeared in 1949. Robert Thacker has drawn attention to her later interest in *Willa Cather's* stories, reminding readers that the librarian in *Carried Away* lists Cather as one of her favorite authors in 1917, and that Munro's story *Dulse* depicts the surrounding of Catheter's cottage on Grand Manan Island, New Bruswick, is a complex invocation and meditation upon Cather. Such a comprehensive history of inter-textual interfaces suggests the crucial importance of reading and writing short stories. For a young woman living on the outskirts of Wingham to escape the constraints of small-town life to gain a sense of power can be comprehended from the following narration:

When I was about fifteen I made the glorious leap from being a fiction of my own ... self conscious miseries to being a godlike arranger of patterns and destinies, even if they were all in my head; I have never leapt back.[22]

Instead of stepping back, Munro has continued to experiment with the short story form, always trying to delineate accurately the complex layering of the way things are or rather the ways things might be assessed from different viewpoints. Her stories initiate the process of trying to make sense out of what happens, though as she remarked on the publication of *Open Secrets, "The older I get (she is sixty-six) the more I see things as having more than one explanation".*[23] While she constantly disproves to theorize about short stories she has on many occasions tried to interpret what a story does, either via the famous *House* metaphor about enclosing space and making connections, or through the medium of metafictional comments within her stories about shifts of emphasis which throw the storyline open to question or structural treacheries.

The Canadian and American publishers represent her *oeuvre* chronologically but with a rearrangement of the order of stories within each collection. Possibly as the review in *Books in Canada* suggests, *"we have to read this as a new presentation in itself, as a narrative on its own, and as a defense of her art",*[25] although it seems unlikely that any narrative of Munro's could exist on its own. The rearrangements within *Selected Stories* would seem to be another example of those characteristic shifts of emphasis which throw the storyline open to question and another statement of Munro's rejection of single or closed meanings in favor of significations which continually shift when events are viewed from different angles.

Certainly Munro's narrative techniques have changed over thirty years, as she allows more and more possible meanings to propagate in every story while refusing definitive interpretations or plot resolutions. In the early collections and whole book story sequences up to *The Beggar Maid* Munro works within the tradition of documentary realism, describing surface details of common life and then disrupting those realistic conventions by shifts into fantasy, suggesting alternative worlds that coexist within the same fictional space.

There is a major shift in Munro's art of storytelling which is reflected in *The Moons of Jupiter* and *The Progress of Love*. In these collections instead of placing the supplement at the end, augmentation pervades the whole narrative through time shifts and shifts in narrative perspective, unsettling the story at every stage of its telling. The story became a series of arrangements, disarrangements and earnest deceptions,where ambiguity and often contradictory meanings have room to circulate in structures of narrative indeterminacy. Her two collections in the 1990s show Munro's engagement with the challenge of how to write stories that will adequately accommodate the indeterminacy and disparate realities observed by her developing self-conscious storytellers. They frequently come upon blankness and secrecy or fantasies and lies, whether they look closely into the present or take a long view over the past. Munro's stories are becoming lengthy and apparently wandering from the subject with so many layers of things going on and crosscutting in time and memory. Ironically, although she has never written a proper novel her short stories blur the distinction between genres, just as they celebrate both imaginary and real life by keeping multiple speculative meanings in circulation.

Alice Munro is down to earth and firmly connected to roots as well as to the many routes that she had travelled. She subscribes to the inner compulsion of the artist that makes her to write what she had decided to write upon, irrespective of form or generic categorization – to take visions as they come and be personally thankful for those that survive. She set some of her short stories in the damp British Columbian metropolis, and the urban geography is so exact that you can practically map the city off her fictions. The most important feature in these stories is that she is the genuinely popular Nobel Laureate who pictures the little sorrows, little joys, little victories and little defeats. By touching upon human nature, she bridges a link between the individual and mankind.

The readers are also actuated by the same motives and passions. Alice Munro's wonderful collections of short stories gain meaning, as the readers gain a glimpse into the spirit of mankind. In the light of various literary and cultural theories, new vistas of the cultural landscapes have opened up to enrich our understanding of life and the world.

Alice Munro beautifully narrates and explains facts about her fiction and her life. When she was in her mid-sixties, she started to take more interest in the Laidlaw side of her family, which she traced back to the Ettrick Valley in Scotland, an area that the 1799 Statistical Account of Scotland labeled as having *No Advantage*. During this period of ancestral interest, Munro travelled in Scotland for a few months, researching the family in cemeteries and public libraries, discovering that in every generation of her family, someone was a writer of letters, journals, or recollections. Munro puts together this material over the years and the material began to shape itself into something like stories. This is not surprising, given that she is, with little or no argument, the best short-story writer currently practicing that underrated art. The combination of the words of her ancestors and her own, she says, resulted in a re-creation of lives about as truthful as the past can be.

Munro's short story writing reveals subtle but definite changes throughout her long career which gives us the pleasures of reading her works. Nevertheless, *Boys and Girls* is representative of Munro's work as a whole, as the formal strategies of the story can be linked to the general trends in her writing. Munro is known for her use of irony, and this story contains numerous ironic flourishes. As the girl protagonist is being groomed to curb her wild behavior and pay attention to her manner of dress and her looks in general, Munro lavishly fleshes out the appearance of the mother, whose labor-intensive housework makes it necessary for her to ignore such things entirely. Thus, as the young girl is trained to be vain, an adult woman is presented whose lifestyle in fact precludes such vanity. The girl's mother ties up her hair and wraps it in a scarf, and favors simple clothing that suits her workaday habits.

Munro has been called a regional writer because many of her stories describe rural Ontario during the Depression era, where Munro grew up, and evoke a bygone time of hardship and deprivation. Munro's protagonists often hold on to their sense of wonder and mystery about the world around them, as does the narrator of *Walker Brothers Cowboy*. The family of the narrator—a young girl—has lost their fox farm, and her father has been compelled to take a job peddling patent medicines, food flavorings, and poisons to the farmers who live in Ontario's countryside, but the girl still looks deeply at the ordinary world and finds enchantment in it. Like many of Munro's works, *Walker Brothers Cowboy* also analyze such universal themes as isolation, identity, and maturation.

Munro further explores these issues in her collection *Lives of Girls and Women*, again from the viewpoint of the narrator of *Walker Brothers Cowboy*. This return to the narrator—Del Jordan—allows interested readers to more closely scrutinize and follow one girl's Endeavour to attain maturity, and observe how her peculiar way of looking at the world influences the choices that she makes. *Walker Brothers Cowboy*, however, authenticates Munro's skill as a writer and her concerns as a woman. Expanding the pattern she had developed in *Lives of Girls and Women*, Munro uses the ten linked stories of *The Beggar Maid* to analyze Rose's personal maturation. But whereas the construction of *Lives of Girls and Women* pivots on Del Jordan's first-person reflections on her efforts to establish emotional and spiritual links with the people around her. The story of *The Beggar Maid* relies on an omniscient third-person narrator to provide insights into the relationships and fissures, connections and reconnections that accumulate and intertwine to shape Rose's understanding of herself and her world.

In her another short story collection *The Love of a Good Woman*, the setting is once again western Canada and the subject matter is secrets, love, betrayal, and the stuff of commonplace things. She takes an ordinary path for delineating these matters. Divided into four parts, it begins with the drowning of a small-town optometrist and ripples outward, touching first the boys who find the body, then a jealous dying woman and her young practical nurse.

Again probing into the silences and dark discretions of provincial Canadian life, Munro shines in her ninth collection, peopled with characters whose sin is the original one: to have eaten of the tree of the knowledge of good and evil. The drama of deathbed revelation is enacted again, between a dying man and the woman at his bedside in *Cortes Island*, when a stroke victim exposes his deepest secret to his part-time caretaker, in what may be the last act of intimacy left to him, and in the process puts his finger on the fault lines in her marriage. In the extraordinary *Before the Change*, a young woman confronts her father with the open secret of his life and reveals the hidden facts of hers; she is unprepared, however, for the final irony of his legacy. The powerful closing story, *My Mother's Dream*, is about a secret in the making, showing how a young mother almost kills her baby and how that near fatality, revealed at last to the daughter when she is 50, binds mother and daughter.

Alice Munro ignores certain important or interesting conventions of short story writing. She knows well even tiny incidents and small details can be the defining ones. She knows that spending a weekend with one's own daughter can be a potential challenge which almost drives you crazy. These stories do not examine the mundane aspects of life we have to cope with most. Alice Munro's stories believe in human dignity and choice. Hers is a moral universe. It's not just the title story which shows us a person making a choice. We tend to just let things happen to us and pretend we are helpless in the sphere of choice. These stories show that sometimes we can. In the world of Alice Munro, the best route is not necessarily the shortest distance between two points.

Some stories of Munro characterized by anti-romanticism even the ones whose plots are based on domestic melodrama as in the description of a baby's near-death in *My Mother's Dream*. This is also true of an adulterous wife in *The Children Stay*. Densely populated, elliptical in construction, each story revolves round its principal events and relationships like planets around a sun. The result is layered and complex, its patterns not always apparent on first reading. Alice Munro probes the everyday sort of person who must make certain choices and live with it. The manner in which she uses language and her graphic description is superb. It will compel you to think surprise and imagine all at the same time. Even a cursory reading of these stories reveals as if these are Munro's problem too. She replaces the brilliant connections and observations she used to make in a paragraph with ten-fifteen pages of incidentals. So much seems like padding. Anyone has a hard time topping themselves as they get older, granted. It is very difficult for any person to write a book like *Open Secrets* in the first place, and it is equally difficult to try and top that.

Royal Beatings, one of Munro's best-known stories, reveals the bonds of love and disdain, cruelties great and small, within a family. Nothing is simple in this story, which features a surprisingly complex plot as well as circumscribed time and tense shifts. It begins late in the depression years in the poorest section of Hanratty, where Rose lives with her father and stepmother, Flo, behind their grocery and furniture repair store. One day Flo relates an incident of a previous thrashing, when three young men attacked the father of the grotesque dwarf Becky Tyde, who sometimes visits the store. The child Rose cannot fit Flo's story together with her present life, for they seem unrelated. Flo's story foreshadows a second beating, this time suffered by the preteen Rose- a ruthless ritual which builds, erupts, and then collapses. When Rose talks back to her stepmother once again, Flo galvanize Rose's father into punishing her. The narrative shifts into present tense to render a horrific account of the first royal beating that cheeky Rose suffers, then switches to future tense to describe the ritual that will follow: a penitent Flo coming to her room to bring an ointment for her back, a tray of food, chocolate milk. Years later, the adult Rose sees a television interview with an elderly man from Hanratty, someone from Flo's story, and is finally able to connect the strands of the past to the present.

Bardon Bus, a collection of eleven stories appears in *The Moons of Jupiter* focuses on the middle aged female protagonists' intense moments in the lives. The beginning of the story sets the tone for what comes afterwards. Had the narrator been an old maid in another generation, she would have perhaps saved a letter and dreamed about an affair while continuing to milk the cows and scour the tin pails. She would have fantasized about surrendering herself completely to a lover who perhaps was a soldier, or a farmer down the road with a shrewish wife and a crowd of children, or a preacher. Though she is of an older generation, and though her actions reflect that, her obsessions are the same. The narrator, writing a book on the history of a prosperous family, is staying in Toronto at a friend's apartment. As part of her research on the family, she recently spent a few weeks in Australia, where she met an anthropologist whom she had known slightly in Vancouver when she was a married college student. She, now divorced, and he, traveling without his third wife, engaged in an affair that, because of the imposed brevity, seems perfect. On returning to Canada, however, she becomes obsessed with him, with the same intensity as the old maid of an earlier generation. The narrator, like other middle-aged women populating Munro's stories, is moderately successful in her career.

Symbolism in Munro's story is very much part and parcel to the thematic structure. In other words, symbols carry half the burden of the stories. The primary symbol in the short story *Boys and Girls* is quite interesting. For example, Flora, the horse, is an important image in the story symbolizing youth, freedom and inexperience. Images of light and dark in her room provide the narrator and her brother with boundaries of safety. During night hours as long as the lights are on, they are safe. Henry Bailey also provides a source of emotional comfort and protection. Delineation of the foxes pens as a medieval town symbolizes the safety and security her father is able to provide, both for the foxes and for her. The narrator feels restricted by inherently female tasks and contrasts directly with the freedom she feels when working outside, like a man.

The fact that the narrator remains unnamed throughout the story could be symbolic of her quest for an identity throughout the story. In this coming-of-age story, the narrator lives in a society that has defined roles for girls. They were expected to be lady-like in their behavior and to learn the skills needed to be a good housewife. At the beginning, the narrator is a tomboy who likes to help her father with the outside work rather than helping her mother with housework. Her mother complains about the narrator's behavior because it's out of character for a young lady. Over the years, the narrator feels the pressures of her mother's grudges and complaints and society's expectations. She starts thinking about her looks, expressing worry whether she'll be attractive. The last trace of her resistance to society's mores are seen when she permits Flora, a horse her father wants to kill, to escape. Her father isn't angry at her because she's only a girl. This statement sums up what society expects of the narrator, and she realizes that she must fit within the confines of that society. As she gets older, the narrator realizes conformity to society's expectations.

In *The View from Castle Rock,* she writes, closer to a nonfictional first person than usual, about traveling the territory with her husband, a geographer, and with special maps sold to accompany a book called *The Physiography of Southern Ontario.* The title sounds almost parodically dry — especially to those Americans who persist in viewing our wild and mysterious northern neighbor as an empire of blandness but in Munro's hands those maps come to resemble poems, runes or magic spells.

Stories of Munro are marked by an authenticity which removes the depression and dullness of the reader. The canvas of her shorter fiction is a record of ancient events. This is indeed the secret of her immense popularity as a short story writer. Norman Mailer, Updike and Roth were the three great male narcissists who dominated the post war realist fiction. But what Munro is unique for is that she is a master at pulling universal truths from even the grubbiest, most gothic farm kitchen sinks and we are right to love her for this exquisite quality. She uses the fictional device to underscore both the subjective nature of storytelling and people's compulsion to use the art of narration to make sense of their lives and to make narrative order out of confusion. Indeed Munro's short stories clearly manifest that story-writing is an art that she has mastered herself with dexterity.

CHAPTER TWO

Her Motive Behind Short Story Writing

Munro began to write short stories with the intention to teach herself to write novels, but since she had to combine writing with caring for her family, she did not succeed in writing a full length novel. This disappointed Alice Munro severely, but her husband continued supporting her and finally she stopped her endeavors of writing a novel and kept on writing short stories. Although she managed to get her stories published in magazines like *The Canadian Forum, Queen's Quarterly, Chatelaine, the Tamarack Review,* and *The Montrealer,* her life as a writer remained difficult since there was no one to publish her stories in book form. This changed in 1968 when her first collection, *Dance of the Happy Shades,* appeared. This collection brought her immediate prestige, respect and admiration; in 1971 she called herself for the first time a writer instead of a housewife. This collection represented the thematic and stylistic characteristics of her stories. The fifteen stories present a perceptive young narrator's dawning awareness of the powerful and legendary shapes lying behind ordinary life in Huron County. Munro's earlier collections tended to consist of linked story series; all are having the same characters or themes. However, in her later collections she prefers unconnected stories, a form which better suits her than the short-story cycle. In explaining the methodology of writing a short story, she says: *"when I write a story I want to make a certain kind of structure, and I know the feeling I want to get from being inside that structure. I've got to make, I've got to build up, a house, a story, to fit around the indescribable feeling that is like the soul of the story. Then I start accumulating the material and putting it together".[i]*

    The Moons of Jupiter is undoubtedly the most crucial turning point in Munro's literary career, for it signified a fundamental change in her narrating methods as she develops new cosmological frame of reference where the stories move between the polarities of the cosmic and the everyday. The very title of this collection indicates a paradigm shift away from maps of the earth to dynamic change and evasive meaning held in ceaseless circulation. *The Moons of Jupiter's* analogy is significant, though these stories do not operate in the stratosphere. On the contrary, as the narrator in the title story remarks on observing the schoolchildren's reactions to the show at the Toronto Planetarium: An effort had been made to get their attention, to take it away from canned pop and potato chips and fix it on various known and unknowns and eerie enormities, and it seemed to have failed.

Munro keeps on locate her stories in landscape of her acquaintances. They are all being with the social landscapes of small Canadian towns and the surrounding countryside of Southwestern Ontario which she has delineated to her readers from the beginning. Her subject matter remains familiar to Canadian pioneer history which is also local history and family history, relationships within families and between generations and perhaps most importantly, the relationships between men and women. As Munro remarked in an interview with Geoff Hancock on the eve of the publication of *Moons*, *"Well, that's the main thing isn't it? This is endlessly interesting and you keep discovering more things about it as a person and as a writer. The whole subject of what men and women want of each other. The big drama of life as I see it right now"*.[ii]

Her subjects and themes have not changed but her narrative methods have. No longer do these stories sit like *Pictures Hanging Together* as they did in *Lives of Girls and Women*, for such a static conception is replaced by a model of endless motion where instability of meaning within any individual story is complemented by the mobile arrangement of the collection as a whole as stories revolve round one another in shifting relationships parallel with the apparently erratic gravitational patterns of the satellites of the planet Jupiter.

The new versatility of conception is crystal clear in this sequence of eleven stories, they do not present the map of a single life but instead a map of many women's lives, each moving on its own axis yet brought by the narrative design into patterns of relationship. When the focus shifts as it so often does, these lives rotate off into darkness as their own independent life cycles continue. Only the first and last stories share the same narrator, she is that Janet Fleming character whose stories Munro separated from Rose's at the last minute in her revisions of the beggar maid.The narration of stories is a variety of women of widely differing ages, from young girls to women in their forties and fifties and even in their eighties, where every woman's story provides a new perspective on all the others. Although the detail of each woman's life story is different, it shares common experience like falling in love, getting married, having children, ageing and dying, so that the focus shifts continually between particularities and universal patterns.

With a focus on the changes brought by time on women's physique and their lives, these stories describe innumerable repetitions and variations in the planetarium. The barely felt gravitational pulls and ironic repulsionsbetween character and stories are a function of the overall narrative design which suggests a wider dynamic transcending any individual's experience, though it is only in the last story that the structure of reference becomes clearly cosmological and mythic.

When we come to the overall arrangement, we see a linear patterning form stories of origin to stories of deaths and endings while along the way stories carve the riddles and mysteries of everyday life. Munro's narrative techniques have always encouraged a plurality of meanings as alternative worlds are positioned alongside each other in the same geographical and fictional scope, but here a new extent is introduced as maps of landscape are overlaid by the mobile maps of cosmology or the complex codes of destiny.

A significant example of this new speculative textual analysis occurs in *Labor Day Dinner* where Roberta and George, the couple who watched the constellations are driving home from a dinner party late at night down the third concession road of Weymouth Township, known locally as the Telephone Road when they are almost run into by a dark green 1969 Dodge traveling at between eighty and ninety an hour approaching from a side road.

It is significant to point the feminine order of meaning that Munro favors here as she shifts the focus from Jupiter to the spinning satellites. Indeed the focus is on mothers of Jupiter till the final story, rather than on fathers and grandfathers, with stories told from the women's perspectives. In the first story Janet rewrites heirs of the living body narrating the stories of the women in her family which have been buried under the claims of stories by and about men. Here patriarchal figures are often discredited, while traditionally feminine roles are shown to be restrictive and damaging or at best cherished romantic illusions. It is only in the title story which is Janet's elegy for her father that mutual love and understanding is acknowledged, at the same time as Jupiter is finally named.

CHAPTER THREE

Description of Life and Reality

The stories of Alice Munro may be located within a realistic framework of reference, though she is always concerned with the shifting significance of events when viewed from different locations in time and circumstance. *Chaddeleys and Flemings* is a mirror story in two parts representing the double strain in Janet Fleming's inheritance, for her grandparents and great-grand-parents immigrated from England and Scotland to Canada in the mid-nineteenth century. It is within this backdrop that Janet looks back in the late 1970s to the 1940s at two important visits in her childhood. The first story *Connection* revolves round a summer visit made by her maternal aunts to her family in the small town of Dalgleish, and the second story *The Stone in the Field* narrates another summer visit made by Janet's family to her paternal aunts on the farms where they and her father grew up. One story faces outwards from Dalgleish to the wider world while the other faces inwards to the secret lives of the unmarried sisters on the farm who, as Janet's modern mother opines, belonged in another generation.In both stories Janet's memories flow in and around her thoughts in the present as she registers changes and continuities between the living and the dead.

The rollicking advent of the four Chaddeley aunts, worldly unmarried women who drive cars and smoke cigarettes, introduces a note of the festivities into the routines of family life in Dalgeish. To a young girl like Janet the aunts are transforming presences, just as their stories about their English grandfather *"What an old snob he was, they said, but how handsome even as an old man, what a carriage,"*[i]transform the past into the stuff of legend.

Janet with her split inheritance cannot totally sympathize with these pretensions even at the time, and she lives to see through this legend when years later she learns about her great grandfather's true origins. Just as the story registers changing interpretations of family history, so the narrative method registers Janet's own changing angles of vision over time.

Accident is a tale of the female romance though it is also story about the role that chance plays in people's lives, for unlike *Labor Day Dinner* there is a fatal accident here with the death of a nine year old boy whose sledge is pushed under a car one wintry December afternoon in 1943 in the small town of Hanratty. The story does not begin with that event however but with the love affair between a young high school music teacher Frances Wright and the science master Ted Makkavala, the boy's father. As the story develops, arbitrariness so pervades the action that we begin to wonder if there are not two accidents here; the road accident and the romance itself, for even Frances suspects that it may be a frail invention.

Both these accidents have far reaching though unpredictable consequences, and the story traces the interwoven effects of both events over a period of thirty years up to the late 1970s when Frances, long since married to Ted and now the mother of two daughters, comes back to her home town for her sister-in-law's funeral. Glancing back over her life, Frances fails to find in it any meaningful pattern at all.

Munro's story again probes shifting perspectives as it relates events from Frances's and Ted's differing standpoints, sometimes in the present and sometimes in the past tense, though always indirectly so that the reader has the sense of being an onlooker who is missing some vital clue. What is clear however is that Tad's vaunted rationalistic viewpoint of the world offers no more explanation for the contingencies of life than France's subjectivised feminine perception? Frances's life story would appear to conform in broad outline to the conventions of a romance plot where she falls in love with a dark stranger and their misdemeanor love affair is finally resolved in marriage after a death and a divorce. Yet the story is infinitely more perturbing than this, for at every turn the design is interrupted to reveal fragments of other repressed stories which are at odds with Frances's version - Ted's Finnish wife's narrative for example, his anecdotes from his past life before he met Frances, and Frances's own skepticism about the every romance plot she has invented for herself. Indeed when Ted unexpectedly makes his proposal of marriage having come to the decision on the spur of the moment when arguing with the head master. This declaration which is traditionally the climax of a love story is so overshadowed by anxiety that Frances is quite terrified at her sudden vision of helplessness and insignificance.

Within the premise of transformation these stories do manage to build images of provisional order, which focus on human behavior, relationships and connections - family connections remembered connections, connections which may have been hidden, which may have been misunderstood or narrowly missed. These connections may be as unlikely as the way the stars tie up into their constellations but nevertheless they are made through the performance of storytelling itself, where like the show in the planetarium, realism is abandoned, for familiar artifice.

The Love of a Good Woman is a murder mystery whose luminous, disturbing power emanates in great part from her transformations of Grimm's Bluebeard tales, compounded with other Grimm tales, Gothic romance, and Bible myths. Munro's power of realistic portrayal is best manifested in these stories, revealing people's lives in exact and mythic detail.

Munro's story *The Love of a Good Woman* begins with a dispassionate yet image-laden and vibrant description of things preserved for the last couple of decades in the local historical museum of Walley, Ontario. These include a red box of optometrist's implements that once, the label tells us, *"belonged to Mr. D. M. Willens, who drowned in the Peregrine River, 1951. It escaped the catastrophe and was found, presumably by the anonymous donor, who dispatched it to be a feature of our collection".[ii]* Then there is a *description* of Willens's ophthalmoscope, with its large and small top disks that could make you think of a snowman, its lenses and hole to look through, handle and electric batteries; then of his retinoscope, with its column from which *"a tiny light is supposed to shine,"* and its flat glass face that *"is a dark sort of mirror. Everything is black, but that is only paint, where the optometrist's hand must have rubbed most often, you can see a patch of shiny silver metal".[iii]*

This present-time prologue is suggestive in tone and, we will later be able to see, conclusion to Munro's Bluebeard and Bible mysteries. Here is the clue that will solve the murder mystery: the red box that escaped the tragedy and was anonymously dispatched some twenty years later. Here are the intimations of a gender and otherwise-transformed Bluebeard tale to come: the victim, the red chamber-box, the hole he looked through. Here are the clichéd images from myth and Bible myth that structure Munro's setting and theme. For example the snowman suggested by the ophthalmoscope's disks is a winter man who will give way to the story's flowerings of spring and summer, childhood and adulthood; and, simultaneously, the snowman warns us of snow jobs—in the socially accepted story of Willens's drowning, and in the Bluebeard stories to come.

Other images include the dark sort of mirror is St. Paul's glass through which we now see darkly. The tiny light that is supposed to shine evokes Christ's Sermon on the Mount and the hymn Protestant children are taught to sing. On the level of the murder mystery, the blackness that is only paint, except where Mr. Willens's hand rubbed, so that a patch of shiny silver can be seen, indicates the sexual rubbings that will lead to murder and dark, cover-up paint. On the level of myth and Bible mystery level, the same image conveys that out of our blackness and rubbing, radiant patches of illumination will come, when we learn to see things in positive framework of mind.

Bluebeard, myths and images come primarily from two Grimm's tales, *Fitcher's Bird* and *The Robber Bridegroom*. The essential Grimm's characters are three: the Bluebeard serial killer, who compels or lures maidens to his isolated dwelling; the dismembered victim maidens; and the surviving clever bride who by daring, trickery, lies and storytelling saves herself and ruins Bluebeard.

The story *Fitcher's Bird* the Bluebeard is an evil wizard, who with his magic touch carries off a first sister, then a second, then a third, giving each in turn an egg to carry always and keep spotless, and a key to a forbidden chamber. Out of curiosity each sister in turn opens the forbidden chamber, where she finds a chopping block and axe, and a bloody basin full of mutilated bodies. Horrified, each of the first two sisters lets her egg slip into the basin; when she cannot wash the telltale blood from the egg, the wizard drags her to the bloody chamber and chops her into pieces. The third, clever sister puts her egg away, explores the forbidden chamber, and heals her two dismembered sisters by gathering and putting in order their severed parts. Tricked by her lies, the wizard loses his power; the clever bride compels him to carry his gold and her sister's home, while she prepares his house for a wedding feast. She places a flower-decked skull in the garret window, and greets the wizard and his friends disguised as a wondrous bird.

In Grimm's *Robber Bridegroom* the clever bride feels a secret horror of her rich betrothed, and marks her way to his dark forest house with peas and lentils. Hidden behind a hogshead by the old woman, the bride sees the cannibal robbers kill and dismember another maiden, whose cut-off finger with a gold ring on it springs up in the air and lands in her bosom. When the robbers fall asleep, the bride and old woman help each other escape to her father's mill. At the wedding feast, the bride tells as if it were a dream her story of the singing bird, the old woman, the murder, and then the dismembering of the other maiden, following each of these four revelations with the tag line, My darling, I only dreamt this, and at the climax producing the cut-off finger with its ring. So her father's guests send the robber and his crew to execution.

Although Munro's four main characters are fully made, fully believable inhabitants of her 1951 Huron County, Ontario, their stories rework much older archetypes, in which the dismembered Grimm elements are brought to life again, reversed, and recombined. The two men, Mr. Willens and Rupert Quinn, are each a Bluebeard and a Bluebeard's victim. Rupert's dying wife, Mrs. Quinn, and her home nurse, Enid, is each a victim and a clever bride; Mrs. Quinn is also something of a female Bluebeard or Atwoodian Robber Bride.

We know Mr. D. M. Willens as a drowned victim before we know him as a Bluebeard character; the first two of the story's four sections only hint at his lady killing ways. A short, hairy, unattractive optometrist in small-town Walley, Mr. Willens is a minor sexual predator who roams the countryside making house calls; sometimes, Mrs. Willens tells the authorities, he gets held up overnight. The full name, D. M. Willens, may be a rough anagram for *demon*. The D. may hint ironically and pathetically at a first name of David, which means beloved.

The grotesque character of Mr. Willens is unloaded by the three young boys who in the spring of 1951, find his body caught in his car in the river, like a muskrat drowned in a trap. They see his arm in its hairy sleeve pushing up through the car's open roof panel like a dark and furry big animal tail.The boys know Mr. Willens as a grotesque, brassy-haired, caterpillar-eye browed cartoon character, short and thick, large of shoulder and head, who in death as in life seems crammed into his little foreign car as if it was a bursting suit of clothes a sort of animal, troll, or cramped giant—or overgrown child. His marriage is childless; Mrs. Willens is a harsh-voiced, androgynously dressed, lumpy little woman and a renowned, generous, shear-carrying gardener, whose house-high forsythia seems like a vision of joyous fertility and sexuality from Katherine Mansfield or Virginia

Woolf.

Enid, the thirty-seven-year-old home nurse who, with her widowed mother, lives next house to the Willens', knows Mr. Willens as a bridge partner who with jokey gallantry, offers her chocolates or a pink rose. Munro's sexual pun is obvious; her subtler pun contrasts the limited romantic possibilities among the Bridges of Huron County with the idealized love affair between a lonely farmwife and a photographer in the American *The Bridges of Madison County*.Whether the Willens's marriage is sexless as well as childless, and whether Mrs. Willens knows about his tomcatting, we cannot know separately and together, the Willens keep up the appearance of vigorous and reasonably happy lives.

Not until the third section of Munro's story, when on 9 July 1951 the dying Mrs. Quinn tells her home nurse, Enid, what happened in her front room, can we clearly see Mr. Willens' death that spring as no accident, no hushed-up suicide, but a Bluebeard-imaged murder. In Mrs. Quinn's deathbed narrative, Mr. Willens becomes an electrified magic-wand version of Grimm's magic-touch wizard, peering into her eye through the hole in his battery powered ophthalmoscope while he kneels like a clumsy, off-balance suitor to grope her bare leg. And Mrs. Quinn, like a mesmerized victim bride, cannot stop him because she has to concentrate on keeping still. This house call which may have been arranged by telephone happens at a time when her husband was supposed to be cutting wood down by the river.

But, almost immediately in Mrs. Quinn's narrative, her groping lady killer lover becomes a helpless victim, down before he knew it, bashed to death in a Bluebeard killing chamber. Rupert, her husband, sneaks in on the two of them when Mr. Willens' hand was on her bare leg: Rupert jumps on the kneeling Mr. Willens from behind *"like a bolt of lightning, Rupert banged his head up and down on the floor, Rupert banged the life out of him".[iv]*Like the severed gold-ringed finger flying through the air in Grimm's Robber Bridegroom, everything flew out of Mr. Willens' knocked-over box. When Mrs. Quinn turns Mr. Willens over, to get him right side up, he is dead or near death; his eyes are neither open nor shut, and dribble pink stuff, like the froth on boiling-down strawberry jam, comes out of his mouth. Although there is no sign that Mrs. Quinn intends to kill the battered Mr. Willens, it is quite possible that he does literally drown when she turns him over: *"he made a sound, Glug-glug and he was laid out like a stone".[v]*

The saga of Mrs. Quinn, then, like that of her precursor Annie Herron in *A Wilderness Station*, is a recognizable but radical transformation of the Grimm Bluebeard tales: Munro's triangle involves one woman and two men, rather than one man and what are essentially two women, the victim and the astute hero; and Munro's essential roles are divided, doubled, shared. Each of the three characters in Mrs. Quinn's killing chamber is some kind of killer and some kind of victim, is basher and bashed and, with genders transcended, some kind of Bluebeard and dismembered or clever maiden. Acting like the hapless Fitcher's brides who cannot wash the red blood from their eggs, and also like the clever bride who puts their dismembered parts in order, Rupert puts things right, and yet cannot put things right. Like a thwarted, overgrown child, he sits bashing himself, pounding on his knees and banging his big flat hands.

It is Mrs. Quinn who, like the practical Lady Macbeth standing by her man, puts the confused killer back together—once she sees that he is not going to attack her. If we go through it slowly, and go beneath the overriding rhythms of Mrs. Quinn's filthy murder tale, we can see how the sudden switch begins quietly, in what child psychologists call parallel play: he jumps on Mr. Willens, she jumps up from the chair, knocking it over. He sets the chair right side up, she gets Mr. Willens *"right side up"* (a position which may finish what her husband started in killing Mr. Willens).[vi]Rupert then sits in the chair where his wife had sat, jumps up as she did, sits again, and pounds himself. Then, trying to spare them both, she covers up Mr. Willens' bloodied head with a tablecloth.

Soon the couple switch into step-by-step, verbal, complementary cooperation, she says to bury him and suggests where, he asks where can they bury his car; she thought of him sitting in his car in the river, he thought up the rest of what to do. She gets the keys to the car from the still warm body and gives them to Rupert; together they carry out the body. Then, honoring the traditional female-indoors and male-outdoors division of labor, she cleans up inside while he drives Mr. Willens' car and body to a nearby little-used road that dead-ends at the river, and pushes them in. Rupert walks back home and tells his wife he did the job in his sock feet, to avoid leaving identifiable tracks; she tells him he *"must have got his brains going again"*.[vii] Both husband and wife, however, are more frightened than they realize, for both leave the telltale dark-red, red-plush-lined box out in plain sight on the front room table, like the Grimm's telltale bloodied egg; Mrs. Quinn finally sees it, many days after the murder, and hides it, in one place and then another; she will not tell where.

Like Lady Macbeth, Mrs. Quinn tries to erase the telltale blood stains. She washes her shoes and the stained floor of the front room and burns the bloodied cloth with which she had covered Mr. Willens' smeared face; she burns her own front-smeared blouse; she paints over the still-stained front-room floor with leftover ugly brown paint. Then, like the Grimm's victims and Lady Macbeth, she goes to pieces. It was the smells of the burning cloth and of the paint that began her fatal sickness, she tells Enid. But, as we can infer from an earlier section of Munro's story, it is more likely that Mrs. Quinn is dying of kidney failure because, as Rupert's nosey, righteous sister suspects, Mrs. Quinn took pills to abort a fetus—probably, as Dennis Duffy has argued, *"Mrs. Quinn thought the fetus was Willens' child."[viii]* This aborted fetus would be a literal equivalent of Grimm's dirtied, bloodied egg.

In this story, what we are told of Rupert and Mrs. Quinn is limited to and colored by what Enid sees, hears, and thinks, as selected, arranged, and reported by Munro's Joycean omniscient-subjective narrator, who shows us only Enid's thoughts. What Enid knows of Mrs. Quinn begins with suspicion, and soon gets worse. A green-eyed, once-pretty young woman, the dying Mrs. Quinn claims to be twenty-seven, though Enid would have thought her older. Rupert's sister, the childless Mrs. Olive Green, who allures the Quinn children and who Enid sees as bent on sniffing out rampant impurity, doubts Mrs. Quinn's Montreal-orphanage story and says she damaged her kidneys by taking pills for an abortion. We learn Mrs. Quinn's first name only after her death, when Enid notes that it is Jeannette, which sounds French-Canadian. Munro's story may seem merely to follow Enid's professional courtesy in referring to her patient as Mrs. Quinn; but the surname pairs Mrs. Quinn and Mr. Willens as mysterious, death-bound, corrupt Gothic elders, in opposition to the younger-seeming, new couple, Enid and Rupert. This effect must be deliberate, as it takes some maneuvering to have Rupert never once use his wife's name.

CHAPTER FOUR

Study of Women Psychology

Every story in the collection *Runaway* revolves round women's thoughts and feelings about themselves and their circumstances. They track the unsteady progress of those thoughts and feelings with great delicacy and precision. In the broadest sense, each of the stories is about a woman acquiring knowledge, about the consequences thereof and about knowing herself. Some of Munro's women are young adults, some are mature individuals looking back on their past and one – in *Trespasses* – is a preteen girl. Indeed, with a single partial exception, the stories are presented entirely from the perspectives of these women. Love, or its absence, is the usual subject matter in the stories, most often between a woman and a man, but sometimes between parent and child. Yet, this topic only partly defines the issues and concerns which the author engages. Munro explores her characters' inner and outer lives with subtlety and nuance, always sympathetically, but with a strong sense of irony and dryness which shades sometimes into a dispassion which is almost ruthless. She does not shy away from exposing her characters to the most painful thoughts and revelations.

Rarely men are in focus in this collection. Only a few are interesting in their own right, but even these are not richly drawn, remaining somewhat shadowy foils for the women whose lives they affect. Most of the male characters are not especially attractive individuals and they are seen only through women's eyes. The absence of fully-developed male protagonists might be viewed as a limitation in Munro, but it is probably a simple matter of artistic choice on her part. It is the women who interest her most and who continually surprise, anguish and delights the reader with their experiences, their pain, their passion, their insights and their awareness.

To analyze and explain Munro's stories is, inevitably, to reduce them shamefully. The characters and their situations are most meaningful in and of themselves, needing no external explication. She is an evocative and complex writer so; one feels a near compulsion to talk, to explain and to share. The first story in *Runaway* is perhaps one least likely to be seriously reduced by comment and analysis. It also introduces themes, perspectives and approaches which Munro develops in different ways within the following stories

The central figure in *Runaway* is Carla, a young lady fixed in a relationship with a moody, rather threatening lover named Clark. She is one of the least sympathetic of the women portrayed in this collection, with her weepiness, her inability to see herself clearly or control her decisions. She is depicted once as seeing herself as captive to Clark and, again, in a scene of crisis, as someone with no existence separate from him. Carla is quite young, so her under-age emotionality and shallow sense of self have not yet undergone the trying fires of experience. The narrative voice of the story alternates between Carla and Sylvia Jamieson, an older neighbor whose husband has recently died after a confining illness, but it concentrates mostly on Carla.

"This was the summer of rain and more rain,"[i] the narrative voice tells us at the beginning of the story, speaking probably for Carla. Sustained rain sets a pervading atmosphere of apprehension and discord. Apprehension that Carla and Clark's boarding and riding stable will fail for lack of customers, and discord between the couple over Clark's plan to blackmail their neighbor, Sylvia. The rain seems to function as atmosphere and symbol, but when it finally breaks, the relief is illusory. Feelings of resolution and renewed happiness for the couple, which the sun brings with it, prove tenuous and probably temporary. It may be that Munro is quietly commenting here on the writer's craft, suggesting that symbols can be too rigid and misleading a guide to understanding.

Munro delineates her characters without illusion as to their weak points. All have certain weak points, although Carla seems especially so, perhaps because only she is at the center of Munro's attention. In an attempt to satisfy Clark and to galvanize their sexual life, Carla has developed a fragmented and fictitious story about how the dying Mr. Jamieson has been stimulated by her and sought her sexual favors during her visits to help with the housework. Carla is now entrapped in her lie, being unable to tell Clark the truth – that she was never even once alone with Mr. Jamieson – even as he forces her to re-visit Sylvia after the death of her husband to set the groundwork for his scheme to blackmail Sylvia into giving him money to keep her well-known poet husband's prestige and name intact.

This rainy summer's agony for Carla is the absence of her pet Flora, a cute and pretty white goat to which Carla has developed a strong attachment, maybe as a counterweight to her increasing uncertain relationship and distress with Clark. Flora has fled away from the stables, adding to Carla's apprehension and discomfort in her relationship. Carla dreams of Flora, a creature which can be seen as representing Carla's earlier, happy, carefree state with Clark or as an object of support or even self-awareness in Carla's apparently fragmented life.

The moment when the narrative makes a sudden shift to Sylvia, we come to know that she, having developed an infatuation with Carla's carefree and rapturous personality, is eagerly awaiting her visit. But that visit goes very differently than expected for both Sylvia and Carla. Carla breaks down under the stress of what Clark expects her to do. Although she avoids telling the older woman about the blackmail scheme, she does, amidst much weeping, tell Sylvia about the loss of Flora and, when pressed, about her unhappiness with Clark. Sylvia takes control of the situation, urges Carla to leave Clark, to run away, and helps make arrangements for her escape. Affected, perhaps, by the wine and food which Sylvia has provided, Carla brightens up, agrees to the plan and eventually boards a bus for Toronto. So, Carla appears to be headed for a new, more self-examined, independent life, and it seems significant that Flora's absence no longer figures in her thinking.

An antithesis occurs almost immediately. While Sylvia is reflecting over the day's events, Carla's new-found composure is coming unglued on the bus. Before she reaches the third stop she has run through a series of recollections and feelings, including a regretting acknowledgment that she has adapted truth somewhat with Sylvia in order to live up to what she imagined to be the latter's expectations of her, as well as increasing self-doubts and an increasingly panicky feeling that she is incapable of living without Clark. She gets off the bus and makes a call to Clark to come.

Now the situation makes a different turn. The sun comes out; the summer is saved for the riding stable; Clark and Carla are in love again; the sex is good. Even a trip which Clark makes to Sylvia's house, apparently to return clothing which Sylvia had given to Carla, but indeed, one doubts, to bully and threaten Sylvia for having urged Carla's attempt at flight, doesn't turn out badly. Just as Clark's presence and talk appear most threatening to Sylvia, Flora reappears all of a sudden in a kind of magical dance, as highlighted in the fog by a passing car's headlights. The mood shifts; Clark is deflected and gives up any plans he might still have been nurturing about blackmailing Sylvia.

The narrative turns yet again in the final section, however. We come to know that Clark did not bring Flora home. In fact, he never told Carla about the goat's appearance at Sylvia's. Carla is astonished, therefore, when she receives a letter from Sylvia mentioning Flora's return. Still, she doesn't act. She is speechless and blank.

After his return from Sylvia's, in bed with Carla, Clark tells her: *"When I read your note, it was just like I went hollow inside. It's true. If you ever went away, I'd feel like I didn't have anything left in me".[ii]*On first reading this, one is compelled to believe in these words positively, as one more nice effect of the sun's coming out. But, upon reflection, it's clear that Clark could just as well be lying to Carla or even threatening her. Munro leaves the meaning obscure. And the story's concluding words are ambiguous as well. While we may realize strongly that Carla is foolish and self-deceived to hold out against temptation, *i.e.*, to seek the knowledge of Clark's motives and her own that might come from finding Flora's bones in the woods, and that she is simply making herself vulnerable to some future abuse from Clark once their new sexual high is over, it is also true that we cannot predict for sure. Carla, like anyone, may eventually find an occasion to seek the truth and to liberate her with self-awareness and self-sufficiency.

Finally, what are we to think about Flora? The pretty white goat is clearly meant to be a symbol in this story. But almost too obviously so, it appears. Disappearing with the rain! Reappearing with the sun! In a mist of magical meaning! Once again it is hard not to suspect an artist's irony on Munro's part. Symbols are fun, she seems to imply, without ever putting it in words, but once again they are a poor guide to understanding.

Runaway may serve as a take-off point for a broader analysis of the stories in the collection. Carla is one type of woman, seen in a particular situation. Munro portrays many others. Juliet, for instance, is the protagonist in three linked stories, *Chance, Soon* and *Silence*. She is a young grad student turned teacher in *Chance*, a still youthful mother visiting her parents with their new grandchild in *Soon* and an older, chastened woman in *Silence*, where the crucial point of the story is Juliet's attempt to deal with the fact that her own daughter has decided to severe all contacts permanently.

There are various equalities between Juliet and Carla. Each pursues love – for both romance and sex – and each makes a leap into a new life. Carla runs off with Clark and Juliet seeks out a man she met only once on a train and from whom she has subsequently received a single letter. Also, Juliet is eventually forced to endure complications in her relationship with Eric, not exactly like Carla's with Clark, but with the similar effect – as revealed in *Silence* – of making her feel miserable and alienated.

Nonetheless, Juliet is very different from Carla, and the crucial situations she faces are different as well. While she shares a youthful uncertainty in *Chance* with Carla, and a self-effacing manner, Juliet is neither repentant nor dependent or living an unexamined life. Even in the first of the three stories she is very much aware of herself and her actions in pursuit of love with Eric. She may be skeptical about the wisdom of her impulsive rush to the North Country to see him, but she knows what she's doing and is willing to face the outcome. Perhaps this is partially because Juliet is a bright, educated woman, someone with special knowledge and a background of reading and study against which she can test herself. This is true, actually, of most of Munro's heroines in this collection and Sylvia in *Runaway* as well, making Carla's stiff and maudlin inarticulateness and helplessness something of an exception to the rule.

The three interlinked stories with Juliet are unquestionably about love, but in the case of the last two, the love which Munro navigates is the love of parent and child. Visiting her parents in western Ontario when her daughter is about a year old, Juliet is surprised and pained in *Soon* to discover a great many previously unexamined aspects of her relationship with them. Her lack of real understanding of her mother and father is anticipated in Juliet's earlier choice of a wildly unconventional Marc Chagall print for her parents' Christmas present. She discovers that picture in the attic when she visits them, and although she's hurt, the knowledge that the Chagall did not speak to them as it did to her adds weight to the gathering evidence that she had not looked truthfully before at her parents' thoughts and feelings. She had been too self-centered to see clearly. The father, Sam, whom she had idolized and respected, is now revealed as weakly conservative about many things, as foolishly attracted to a girl who is helping out about the house and as less devoted to his wife than Juliet had always imagined.

Most of Munro's heroines are familiar characters who seem very real to the reader and who are brought especially close to us by their simplicity and ordinariness and by Munro's habit of punctuating scenes of high emotion or dramatic import with colloquial expressions of everyday, north-American use. There is always a sense of irony in this, of course, but the reader cannot help feeling disarmed as well, drawn more closely to the characters and encouraged to feel even more strongly the extent to which those characters' thoughts, feelings and experiences are reflections of her or his own.

Powers is the last story in this collection, a challenging work in which the author once again analyses motifs and strategies which she has investigated before. One might even say that *Powers* helps put the rest of the collection in perspective by focusing certain themes and approaches. There are some techniques and tools, we have not seen previously, such as the use of diary entries and letters, segmenting the story into five titled sections and the use of a male character's perspective for part of the story. Nevertheless, it is the commonality of *Powers* with its sisters in *Runaway which* is most appealing and, perhaps, scintillating.

Munro develops her chief protagonist gradually and deliberately, first of all with hints and suggestions from the youthful Nancy's own diary entries and from letters she writes as a young woman, as well as from comments made by Ollie, a young man her own age who is her husband's cousin. Nancy impresses us as a bright, impulsive woman, self-centered and conventional certainly, a bit condescending and rather reckless about other people's feelings. However, Ollie is probably unfair in blatantly portraying Nancy as pampered, saucy, and egotistical because she does express hints of self-awareness about her weaknesses from the beginning. Unfortunately, that sense of self-awareness is not nearly strong enough to prevent her from accepting a feeling less but conventionally happy marriage to the older wife or from casually showing off her acquaintance, Tessa, to Ollie by descending on her home and insisting that Tessa exhibits her special psychic powers by telling Ollie what he has in his pockets. When Tessa succeeds, Nancy gets the satisfaction of seeing that Ollie is greatly impressed. Still, when he questions her about Tessa on their walk home, he causes her to wonder – but only very briefly –whether she hadn't been at fault in showing Tessa off like a freak.

The plot of *Powers* unfolds continuously in the first and second sections, but forty-one years go by between the second and third sections. Now Nancy is about sixty-three, with a husband suffering from dementia. Having just received word of Tessa for the first time in many years, she visits a private hospital where Tessa has been incarcerated for decades. Forty years ago Tessa had agreed to run off with Ollie, thinking he loved her and was proposing marriage, in order that they might investigate her psychic powers in a scientific way. Now Tessa tells Nancy that Ollie is gone; she believes that he's dead, because she saw him so in her mind's eye after she was committed to the hospital and because he has never come to rescue her.

The last two sections of *Powers* vindicate our view of Nancy, but in a different and painful way. Sixty-seven years old, a widow now, returning from a cruise meant to help her recover from Wife's death, Nancy meets Ollie, totally unexpectedly, on the streets of Vancouver. She says nothing to him about what she learned from Tessa, even though it is sharply in her mind, and Ollie lies more directly by describing how Tessa died years ago and how he spread her ashes in the Pacific. They both paste over the truth with pleasant conversation, and once more our previous evaluation of Nancy is vindicated. She's still vain, she's still bound by convention, and she can still be bright and sarcastic when on display.

The conclusion of *Powers* makes one think of parallel situations or experiences in the other stories, of other moments in which a flash of truth or recognition comes to a character, or in which, sometimes, Munro brings that flash of illumination directly to her readers.

With the echo of Munro's words in our ears, this is a very good place to end. We are reminded yet again that this author, like all others, speaks best for herself. There are common threads of experiences among the stories which may be commented on, to be sure, and there are points of explication which may be helpful, but in the end each story is an exquisite and powerful navigation, utterly unto itself.

conclusion

Throughout the chapters of this book I have systematized and studied, in critical terms, a range of Alice Munro's short stories as an expression of my conviction that the imaginative, fictional sphere in her oeuvre does not operate as an addition or opposition to what is real. Rather, this domain exists as a dimension on the either side of reality as its possibility. The jolt of sudden materializing patterns in the sphere of the real, enigmatic or not, becomes a source for storytelling. In the stories, we come across with a familiar world that does not appear unusual or its circumstances inexplicable until someone thinks of endeavoring to make a narrative out of them. When we attempt to understand the deeper meaning of the real, it reveals itself in its full mysterious glamour. In *Post and Beam* as in so many of Munro's stories, the charm for these captivating patterns and secretly lurking forces of life has priority over subjective suffering.

The short stories of Alice Munro are character-based. But her characters give way to something vaster and more enchantingly elusive. Munro's protagonists are not heading towards destiny, but vice versa. In carnal affairs, fate is not a matter of lovers finally finding each other and fitting together, but of seemingly insignificant life-factors establishing fatal courses that permit existences to intersect. Such aspects often come to givenness as features of a personality or of behavior, but are not reducible to these. Munro's concept of fate is not Thomas Hardy's lurking inescapable determinism, nor is it the ruthless arbitrariness of Albert Camus. Instead, it appears as an inescapable or undeniable possibility that liberates the protagonists. A significant number of Munro's stories are based on the theme of love. These stories show a surprise and excitement at this a-personal concord in the attraction between lovers or potential lovers. More frequently it is there in a brief moment of an eventual turn, as in the ceremonious bolting of a door in *The Children Stay* or *Accident* or as in the fullness of the kiss between Jinny and Ricky in *Floating Bridge* reminding us of the cool or starry kisses in *Nettles* and *Comfort*. These ensuing moments do not reconcile with the protagonist's lives as they grow, but are sources of a hopefulness that I see as pervading Munro's fiction. In premises where the stuff lives are filled with threatens to be nothing but rubble or rubbish, these moments are resources that are reverberant in the promise of content and meaning.

All of this pre-supposes a disengagement from the subjective. In a screening-away of relational thinking, Brendan, the relational hub of Lorna's existence, can therefore not be included in the world where relations are replaced by dashes and meaning by compellation.

This phenomenon of detachment from the personal is more or less prominent in all of Munro's stories. Without this tilt to sheer away from subjective goals, final elucidation or simplistic pledges, the protagonists would not be adjusted to the compelling forces that lift them into their various and different possibility-spaces. It is the fatal coursing of an event that is in focus here, not a revelation of a preset destiny.

During the growth of Munro's narratives, it is easy to overlook the significant role played by time and the directedness of time. *Post and Beam* only makes sense as a particular sequence of acts and events, and the same goes for the faint impressions; on the sidewalks. They imply movement, not simply in space, but also in time. All the mentioned leaves have not fallen or been plastered at the same time. The imprints of feet in uncertain bird tracks have been left one after the other, just as spring required to follow autumn in order for the leaves to appear as shadows rather than as leaves. Spring does not follow autumn by means of some decision, but by way of necessity. This sense of a necessary coursing of things, and of humans being trapped in time's inevitable progression, is foundational in *Post and Beam*. The prominence of necessity is highlighted by the phrase that is central to the story will not have happened. Feeling guilty about the way Polly has been treated during the unexpected stay in her home, Lorna suddenly feels certain that this bereft cousin has taken her life. If the vision of Polly's body reclining lifelessly against the kitchen door is true, there is nothing Lorna can do to save her, and her keenness to get back to Polly from a brief trip out of town is pointless with respect to the factual coursing of acts and events. Yet Lorna wishes to speed as urgently as possible towards the deed that has or has not occurred, as if the permanence of its necessity were lying in the future rather than in the past. On the one hand, the words have happened refer to a compulsory requirement that, if it is real, is buried spontaneously in the past. She tries to tell herself to be calm and rational instead of hysterical and over-imaginative. The words 'have happened' refer to a necessity that falls slightly short of being absolute by lying in the hands of God. On the way back in the car to the hypothetical suicide scenario, Lorna furtively pushes herself into the extreme position of believing that it was possible, up to the last minute it was possible to make a bargain. In a story that is replete with of passing references to religion, this settlement is theological in nature. There is an apparent parallel to Jephthah and his daughter from The Book of Judges where he makes a pledge to the Lord to offer the first person that meets him at his victorious return from the Ammonites. To Jephthah's dejection, this person is his beloved and only daughter. Lorna's settlement, in which she snatches away any thought of her children, refers to a deal she might want to make with an omnipotent God, strong enough to alter the movement of eventual lines that have already taken place.

References

Chapter 1

1. H. Horwood, Interview with Alice Munro, in J. Miller (ed.), *The Art of Alice Munro: Saying the Unsayable* (Ontario: University of Waterloo, 1984) p. 123-35.

2. Munro Alice, *What Is Real?*, in J. Metcalf (ed.), *Making It New: Contemporary Canadian Stories* (Toronto: Methuen, 1982). In J. Metcalf and J.R. (Tim) Struthers (eds), *How Stories Means* (Erin, Ontario: Porcupines Quill, 1993), p. 331-4.

3. Munro Alice, *Lives of Girls and Women* (Harmondsworth: Penguin, 1982) p. 249.

4. Alice Munro, *The Moons of Jupiter* (Harmonds-worth: Penguin, 1984) p. 27.

5. Alice Munro Interview, in G. Hancock, Canadian Writers at Work (Toronto: Oxford University Press, 1987) p. 191.

6. Munro Alice, *White dump, The Progress of Love* (London: Flamingo, 1988), p. 308.

7. Munro Alice, Author's Commentary on *An Ounce of Cure and Boys and Girls*, repr. Metcalf and Struthers, p. 185-7; quoted by Catherine Sheldrick Ross, *Alice Munro: A Double Life* (Toronto: ECW Press, 1992) p. 45.

8. Stephen Smith, Interview with Alice Munro, Quill & quire (August 1994) p.1.

9. Dennis Duffy, *Something She's Been Meaning to Tell Us, Books in Canada*, 25:9 (December 1996), 8-10.

Chapter 2

i   Ross, Catherine Sheldrick. *Alice Munro: A Double Life* (Toronto: ECW Press, 1992) p.65.

[ii]Alice Munro Interview, in G. Hancock, Canadian Writers at Work (Toronto: Oxford University Pres, 1987), p. 222.

Chapter 3

i   Munro Alice, *Moons of Jupiter*, (Harmonds-worth: Penguin, 1982) p. 8.

[ii]Munro Alice, *The Love of a Good Woman* (New York: Knopf, 1998) p. 3.

[iii]Ibid., p. 3,4.

[iv]Munro Alice, *The Love of a Good Woman: Save the Reaper* (New York: Knopf, 1998) p.57.

[v]Ibid., p. 57,58.

[vi]Ibid., p. 57,58.

[vii]Ibid., p. 61.

[viii]Ibid., p. 182.

Chapter 4

[i]Munro Alice, *Runaway* (New York: Alfred A. Knopf, 2004) p.4.

[ii]Ibid., p. 42.

[i]Munro Alice, *Runaway* (New York: Alfred A. Knopf, 2004) p.4.

[ii]Ibid., p. 42.

Bibliography

Primary Sources: Books By Munro

- Munro Alice, *Lives of Girls and Women* (Harmondsworth: Penguin, 1982) .
- Alice Munro, *The Moons of Jupiter* (Harmonds-worth: Penguin, 1984) .
- Munro Alice, *The Love of a Good Woman: Save the Reaper* (New York: Knopf, 1998) .
- Munro Alice, *Runaway* (New York: Alfred A. Knopf, 2004).

Secondry Sources:

- H. Horwood, Interview with Alice Munro, in J. Miller (ed.), *The Art of Alice Munro: Saying the Unsayable* (Ontario: University of Waterloo, 1984).
- Munro Alice, *What Is Real?*, in J. Metcalf (ed.), *Making It New: Contemporary Canadian Stories* (Toronto: Methuen, 1982). In J. Metcalf and J.R. (Tim) Struthers (eds), *How Stories Means* (Erin, Ontario: Porcupines Quill, 1993).
- Alice Munro Interview, in G. Hancock, Canadian Writers at Work (Toronto: Oxford University Press, 1987).
- Munro Alice, Author's Commentary on *An Ounce of Cure and Boys and Girls,* repr. Metcalf and Struthers; quoted by Catherine Sheldrick Ross, *Alice Munro: A Double Life* (Toronto: ECW Press, 1992) p. 45.
- Stephen Smith, Interview with Alice Munro, Quill & quire (August 1994) p.1.
- Dennis Duffy, *Something She's Been Meaning to Tell Us, Books in Canada,* 25:9 (December 1996), 8-10.
- Ross, Catherine Sheldrick. *Alice Munro: A Double Life* (Toronto: ECW Press, 1992) p.65.

www.ingramcontent.com/pod-product-compliance
Lightning Source LLC
Chambersburg PA
CBHW051423250726
48655CB00003B/1213